Fothermather

Gail McConnell

Published by Ink Sweat & Tears Press
London SW12 8DG
inksweatandtears.co.uk

© Gail McConnell 2019
Series editors: Kate Birch and Helen Ivory
Typeset by Starfish Limited
Printed and bound by Page Bros, Norwich

Seahorse cyanotype by Margo McNulty

Virginia Woolf, *A Writer's Diary*, Ed. Leonard Woolf. London: The Hogarth Press, 1953. The Society of Authors as the Literary Representative of the Estate of Virginia Woolf.

D. W. Winnicott, 'Hate in the Counter-Transference' *The International Journal of Psycho-Analysis* (1949; 30:69-74). By permission of The Marsh Agency Ltd on behalf of © The Estate of D.W. Winnicott 2019.

Francis Ponge, 'Notes pour un coquillage', translated by C.K. Williams, 'Notes Toward a Shellfish' and Francis Ponge, 'Bords de mer', translated by Margaret Guiton, 'Seashores' in Francis Ponge, *Selected Poems*, Ed. Margaret Guiton. Winston-Salem, NC: Wake Forest University Press, 1994.

'Now' is after 'Snow' by Louis MacNeice from his *Collected Poems*, published by Faber & Faber.

Grace Paley, 'Mother' in *The Collected Stories*. London: Virago, 1999.

Changeling: A Memoir of Parents Lost and Found by Sandra Newman (© Sandra Newman, 2010).

Sigmund Freud, translation from *Das Unbehagen In Der Kultur (Civilisation and its Discontents)*. Vienna: Internationaler Psychoanalytischer Verlag, 1930.

ISBN 978-0-9927253-4-1

For Finn

– who made me a parent –

&

for my fothermathers

Fothermather by Gail McConnell is the product of the seventh Café Writers Commission. The Commission is supported by Kate Birch and Dominic Christian and held in conjunction with poetry webzine *Ink Sweat & Tears* whose print section publishes the pamphlet. Each winner receives £2000 and 100 copies of their collection.

The judges of the 2017 Poetry Pamphlet Commission Competition were Kate Birch, Chris Gribble (Chief Executive of the National Centre for Writing, Norwich) and poets Jay Bernard and Helen Ivory.

Contents

Introduction   9

Orange   11
what is that sound?   12
light the seahorse   13
when I see your spine   14
your shape is a letter   15
Talk Through the Wall   16
Shell Notes   17
Ashore   18
Res   19
In *The Argonautica*   20
Now   21
Cuttlefish   22
Captain Calamari   24
Untitled / Villanelle   25
I cannot think   26
~~I cannot think~~   27
Fothermather   28
me : : he   30
An Apple Seed   32

Acknowledgments   33

Introduction

Last year I became a parent to Finn, the brilliantist. My partner carried Finn in her body and feeds him with that body. I carried Finn the only way I knew how – in my imagination and in the bodies of poems. For all the consideration we've given to fluidity and letting go the binaries, the language of parenthood – mother and father – remains oddly fixed. And the sameness perceived in 'same-sex' partnerships of 'two mothers' doesn't allow for differentiation. My initial ambition was to examine non-biological queer parenthood, asking what queerness does to parenthood, and parenthood to queerness, and how we might imagine parenting without gendering it so rigidly in name and form.

Then Finn came along and changed everything forever. My interest shifted from how Finn might name *me*, to how anybody names anything and is named at all. I grew more curious about how sounds are made; how language happens; how meanings cleave; how forms are improvised and adapted in creaturely communication; and how it all occurs in relationship: the I-you-me entanglements by and through language happening in poetry. *Fothermather*, a nonsense word that tells the truth, first appears in 'Untitled / Villanelle', a poem at once untitled – not (yet?) named, perhaps seeming unentitled – and named by its form. It hinges on these states. As do I. In the back of my ear was Seamus Heaney's 'Fodder', where wordplay makes audible linguistic colonization and intimate familial naming. 'Mather' comes from *meadar* in Irish, related to the Latin *metrum*, which carries a vessel for measuring and poetic metre. *Fothermather* becomes an alphabet I play with in its formative parts, sounding it out syllable by syllable, along with Finn.

Our family has come into existence in Northern Ireland where – at the time of writing but hopefully not much longer – same-sex marriage and abortion are illegal, there is no NHS fertility treatment for same-sex couples, and their adoption success rates are 1 in 15 compared to 1 in 2* in the rest of the UK. Although same-sex marriage is now legal in Ireland, procedures do not yet exist to allow me to sponsor Finn's citizenship as his Irish parent – only a biological parent will do. This context has been formative in numerous ways. Yet most formative of all, now, is Finn. Like Finn, these poems are busily at play – with gender, attachment, carrying, queerness and creaturely life.

*Siobhan Fenton, 'Same-sex adoption rate lowest in UK'. BBC News NI. 14 Dec 2018.

Orange

There must be many ways to peel an orange. And by orange I mean Tangerine. Or Clementine. The pocket-sized fruits best not pocket-stored. With these one can fashion a spiral. Or: witness the teenage boy make testes and a penis before segmenting the fruit. With the orange itself, you're into the business of marking the skin – the knife's continuous line – then peeling it back to reveal the flesh and pulling it off in great husks, the cuts on your palms all stinging. 'I have worked myself too dry this time. There is not one idea left in the orange.' So wrote Woolf as though thinking of Ponge, who sees the orange seed as a miniature lemon.

We broach it first in bed, this question of sperm. You rule out Danish blondes. Alone, I tick things in the pull-down menus. Caucasian. Dark hair. Green eyes. Five five to five nine. Fermin appears. His true name I'll never know. It takes me back to the three-legged cat we had in Georgia, Mr. Joshua Ingalls. When the time came to cross the sea, we took him to the shelter. They renamed him Fiesta. He is Spanish. He does not use prescription lenses. He does not suffer from any allergies, medical conditions or physical abnormalities. I listen to his voice. I see his baby photos. I read his handwriting, profile, Q&A, Emotional Intelligence Test, family tree. He is a saint. He rolls an orange – Navel, say, or Blood. He rolls it round. Round beneath his palm as the bulls run through the streets. It's alphabetical, I know. After Fiesta, Guy or Gabriella or Giggles. But seeing meaning in the sequence can be hard to resist. The first orange tree in France came from Pamplona. This fact I give you with a glass of juice. I have read too much and wish I could unknow the things I seem to know. To hold.

Why does the mother hate her child? Winnicott starts an alphabet, beating Mr. Ramsay and making it to R. 'His excited love is cupboard love, so that having got what he wants he throws her away like orange peel.' It is morning. As my lover opens her mouth, making the awww sounding shape I thought might be orange, I see it might be ovum. What can I give her, having neither seed nor egg, or not the egg she needs? Do I want to be the mother thrown away like orange peel? Will I be so hated and, withstanding it, so loved? Or will I be a different mother, whose body has not been a room, whose breasts contain no nourishment, who feeds our child with Honeybells, Tangelos, Satsumas, Mandarins, Lane Lates, Summer Golds, Cara Caras? Child, if you come, you will be twice loved. My love will carry you, and I will be the one who peels for you the Minneola, gives you it in segments.

what is that sound?

                                    waves
sounds   rise   crash   rise   repeat
                              waves sounds
rise crash rise repeat repeat
                          waves sounds rise
crash rise repeat repeat
                    waves sounds rise crash
rise repeat repeat
waves   sounds   rise   crash   rise
repeat repeat
waves

who is that sound?

light

a photic   bobbing
the   in   zone
lives
seahorse

head
of a
h
o
r
s
e

belly of a   kang
ar
oo

t
a
i   key
l   on
of a m

I am neither   the female Seahorse who lays the eggs,
nor   the male Seahorse who carries them.

I am   not quite either and a little of both.

whoyou whoyou whoyou ?

13

when I see your spine – when I see that,
    yes, you have a spine! –
        my mouth sounds

          S
          e
          a
          h
          o
          r
          s
          e

        in the dark
      gazing at the blackness of the screen
& at these flecks of white / of light / your bones

          e
          s
          r
          o
          h
          a
          e
          S

a creature with a spine
    turning upside down / the right side up for birth
eyes and lines are measuring
    each limb in turn
1, 2, 3, the chambers 4

        O
        Seahorse
        bobbing
        darkling
        deep

           O seahorse who is not upright
           who nuzzles at the seashore O

                    deep
                  darkling
                  bobbing
                  Seahorse
                    O

your shape is a letter, yeS
   a letter shaped by us?
I read you as unravelling B
   with the coiling
      tail of g

§

As a sea-turn brings a breeze or gale
   that mists or clouds or makes us move,
your nature's rearranging what we thought
   we knew biology or artifice might prove.

You understand that camouflage is custom, true
and changeable in circumstance, and that a name
obscures as much as it contains. O fish! O fish
with spine and neck. Born of choice and chance,
born of the male, a vertebrate upending expectation.
You're a question mark reversed & beautifully embellished.

§

You're made of rings, not ribs. Spiralling your way.
   Sea-plants are your hitching posts, tail twisting
      round the stem. Pleasant, being tethered.

Talk Through the Wall

you say you   think you feel you   might be able just   to sense the
    baby bubbles   that's the feeling   bubbles on the   walls like bubbles
pressing up   against the sides   & popping at the   line the books
    say they're too wee for kicks   or stretching pushes to be

felt to register inside   your skin but   but you're sure   you think you're
    feeling something like their   contact something   giving shape to this
arrangement something   annotating what   this is all

    happed up in   a caul & tapping   out negotiations   little one starts
wiggling the eyebrows they now   have & testing   out their joints to see
    the bends   of elbows knees   & toes of waving hands   of kicking
feet of tilting   head of shifting   hips of curling   tongue of fingertips

    with fingerprints already   grooved therein   of taking to the mouth
the thumb of testing   out all texture   & of placing fingers on
    this fine-haired skin   their covering   as flexing limbs find boundary

lines know   what it is to be   inside to be   within to grow
    attached though not to me   through blood & cord   we make another
way to fasten   each to each   nightly I speak   with you talk through
    the wall about the day   & tell you of the work I did   or didn't do

& read you rhymes   like London   Bridge is broken down   though who is
    this gay lady   who's rebuilding   it with iron & steel with iron   & steel that
bends the dance   goes on returns repeats   dance o'er my Lady Lea dance

    o'er the three   or four or five ply yarn   spun out for   you in air
to jump before it   sweeps the ground I burble on   in skipping songs
    in chants that come that come   & go from the bottom   of the deep
blue sea sea   sea with a heel   a toe   & a barley   O

Shell Notes

Parented by 'Notes Toward a Shellfish', C.K. Williams' translation of Francis Ponge, 'Notes pour un coquillage'. 'Shell Notes' is a rearrangement of this source.

Look – this multi-chambered skull is spectral
at sea. It shelters (and gives pleasure as a dwelling
to) a not-too-social mollusk. Anything –
the amorphous to the form; what is colossal
to the small (the giant over David; the cathedral
to the dust) – any sort found differing
can make for uneasiness in a being.
Animal, fish and human like a shell.

Form is adapted from else where (a residue
of that place it bears). Glass from sand, city
from stone, a well out of the ground, a statue
made of bone. Sculpted things, inconceivably
there, show through at last. Adjustment is true
genius. Less man from ape, than *boy* from body.

Ashore

*An erasure poem from 'Seashores', Margaret Guiton's translation of Francis Ponge,
'Bords de mer'.*

           she nears her limits   repeating
      wave by wave

     a   thinning out   –   also
            immensity –

     wide
                     vigorous muscle
                                stretches
out

                    first   formed
  by   boundless   wave

                              someone

climbing
                    bare   head

                          labial

               shores
deliver   mingled
    rivers   –

Res

An erasure poem from 'Seashores', Margaret Guiton's translation of Francis Ponge, 'Bords de mer'.

                                        thing

her   the   thing

       on

   the   table

        knives

                              the blade

  Out   in

out

    An elementary concert

                    the first

                  a   someone

                        uttering   all

           uttering

              itself

                addressing

     us

             —

                  the anarchy of

        matter

In *The Argonautica*, a seahorse bounds out of the sea
and is read as a portent: a sign that it is time to lift the ship
and walk through the desert in the creature's traces.

We are given a baby bath, breast pumps, a black bin bag of fifty
babygros, nipple cream, breast pads, toys, a side sleeper, black and
white books and a cot. One thing I buy is a Captain Calamari.
Pregnancy takes us into an alternative economy – a secret zone of
borrowing and gifts from almost-strangers. It is so unlike the weird
necessity/privilege of a queer couple in NI spending money
in the private fertility industry, in the hope of what that industry calls 'a
live birth'. Then again, this process has been made possible through
the 'donation' of something we were without. I had not anticipated
seeing sperm as a gift.

The sailor of, or in, the ship is the argonaut. (We are carried by your being.)
Argonaut is also the name given to the paper nautilus, a cephalopod mollusk.
The female has webbed sail-like arms. She makes a thin, coiled,
papery shell in which the eggs are laid.

I cannot feel your kicks and strokes   these are the pages of your becoming
I have the texture of these notes   as your becoming is occurring

Before I held you for the first time, your cord still attached, were twenty-four difficult hours.

After the birth trauma counsellor said *hippocampus*, I started to remember them.

§

your flesh against my flesh is the best feeling I have ever known

Now
after Louis MacNeice

The room was suddenly you
                          and the great bay-window I pressed
palms to as a child came whippling back
                              beyond the spawning factory you started in
your mother plump with eggs they counted out
                      in snow and hush the embryos collateral: a key
ring compass rose revealing cardinal directions wordlessly
        happening this instantly and yet to be formed us –

paper gowns and paper hats and silver shining scales
   machines beep beep and spit out sheets
scribbling to chart your heart inside the shell and out
   of it into this theatre room fluorescence

with a bubbling sound for world
              whawha whawha whawha
                                  is come
   on the ears on the ears on the ears on the ears –
you   petal delicate pink-cheeked and damp between our hands.

Cuttlefish

1

Cuttlefish, cuttlefish,
cuttlefish is not a fish –
bone-hard as a butter dish
the shell that keeps you buoyant-ish.

You look as if you've sneezed
up your insides and now they're hanging
from your nose, if nose you have –
they dangle from your face and form it too.

Your eyes – drunk W's – miss nothing
(though nothing shows in colour)
in front, behind and through the dark

the pattern of your pigment cells
settles first on zebra, then on saddleback,
then on 1980s neon.

2

The female seems standoffish.
The male looks down. He'll re-

furbish the structure of him-
self, and take his boyish limbs

(his telltale eight) & (tucking)
make one pair vanish

& then approach
the one he wants, dragging

skin and sac and bone
by rippling his skirts –

skirts enclosing (in a doubled fold)
the ink bag, hearts and gills

and the anus usually not featured
in rhymes about God's creatures.

3

Wiki makes a pineapple of you when dead
and splayed in bird's-eye view. *Two long prehensile tentacles*
   (those grasping bits)
hang down like plaits, though really more like snakes
with heads. With eyes. With dotted mouths.
   They've made you part-Medusa,
part-pine-cone-fleshy-fruit.

The queen of -ish.
   The queen
of blending in / The king
of bending rules
   governing
colour, shape & partnership.

To be with the one you wish for – touching, cloak to cloak,
   and bone to bone – you grow identical
at least in part. The same game lets you hide.
With a greyish, bluish, skirt-swish,
      goes the cuttlefish.

Captain Calamari is an eight-limbed octopus with an eyepatch, a crinkly hat and a mirror on her bottom. Despite the name, she is not a squid served as food. She is more like a pen-fish, holding and wielding ink. The OED gives calamary as the general name for Cephalopods or Cuttle-fish of the family Teuthidæ, whose internal shell is 'a horny flexible pen'. What a way of being. Of living.

On the same day we go to the labour workshop, I go to a talk about *Our Living Seas*. My laminated posters of *Northern Ireland's Ocean Giants* get mixed up with the *Dilation Wave Diagram* and *Water Birth* notes.

This is the first time I see Finn
from *fionn*
also being fin

fin meaning feather meaning
wing meaning flight
meaning swim
as a fish fin one's
way fin a passage

through the deep fin on
down fin along
a way to
steer propelling
argos meaning swift

shining bright the
motion causes
flickering and
glancing light
fionn meaning white

meaning bright clear
and fair meaning
ascertain discover
on the white
crested waves of the sea

what is the *and* between you and I?
and is the what between you and I

Untitled / Villanelle

'I have often longed to see my mother in the doorway.' - Grace Paley
'Because having a father made me want a father.' - Sandra Newman

I have often longed to see my mother
tap-dance in a top hat like she did before he died –
having (had) a father made me want a father.

A mather / madder / mether is a measure
that keeps its shape & holds what's stored inside –
I   often   see my mother.

Mistype the word it stretches to a fother
(a cartload carries fodder, hitched outside) –
                a father made me.

You come to know the one against the other.
You measure till the meanings coincide.
I have often longed to see my father.

My mother's mother died before her daughter was a mother.
Alone, she gave me all she could provide –
(not) having a father made me want (to be) a father.

What am I to you? Mother? Father? Neither?
Like cells, names split & double, unified.
I have often longed to   mother
mother father fother mather matherfother fothermather

I cannot think of any need in childhood as strong as the need for a father's protection.

I   a   child

I   think of   father

I cannot think of   h   e   r

                                        d a

                                                    for   t

I   not   I

          h   e   r   e

        not   h   e   r   e

I   a   father

                need

                                        d a

                                        d a

Sigmund Freud

o   O   oO   o   o   O   o

                                                                              i n

                                      the

          o   c   e   a   n

I can   fo   ther

c   o   n   ne   c   t
 a   t t   a   ch

   h   o   ld   f   a   s   t
                    as the

               s   e   a
           h o   r   s e

...........o...........O...............................oO.........o...........................o.....................O......o

Fothermather

An Anagrammatic Story

fothermather
form & matter

    mote & atom
    earth & ether

        heart & ear
        foot & feather

            fate & farther
            – metre
                tremor

                    meteor?
                  Thor?

              fear harm
            retreat retreat

        retort & tether
        fort & moat

      mar the ream
      tear the tome

    form a rath
from earth form O

        or or or
        teem the moat

        or or or
        the
        heart
        free
        more

        or
        or
        or
        o teeter-totter o o o

form a raft
ro ro ro

from the reef
oar forth o'er foam

err here & there
roam fore & aft

at fathom three
a tar
– hear hear

at three
me hear the mort

father: hero or threat?
for them, father a foe

them arm
rearm

•

atom

met the

heart

afore –
he father me

after –
hate / reform

mother mother
there for me?

mother fothermather me

me :

ha ha ma ma
hee hee fo fo

ma ma me form
me form ma ma

me fathom he
he fathom me

me form other
me form ta ta

them form me
me form them more

from me to he
from there form troth

ma ma me form
ah ha ma ma

he her me
here fathom three

ha ha ma ma
hee hee fo fo

her he her
to & fro

: he

ha ha ma ma
hee hee fo fo

he form ma ma
ma ma he form

he fathom me
me fathom he

he form other
ta ta he form

he form them
them more form he

from he to me
troth form therefrom

form me ma ma
am am ah ha

me her he
three fathom here

ha ha ma ma
hee hee fo fo

her he her
fro & to

An Apple Seed

apple   cup   &   shell
I say these things to you   I read them
from the   book   book   book   this is   a

book   you roll yourself to where
the sound must be   to sound to word to thing
to me the mouth that sounds out ssssssssshhhhhhhh

ell   you watch my lips to see the shell
come out   come out shell the shell
comes out & curls itself around the air

again the thing   itself is waves
of sound   for sound it is a swimming
moving to & fro   vibrating shell

the peel & rind   creaturely home   upon a time
spacetime is soft-bodied
Einstein said   *the mollusk*   we are in   a constant

flux   the quantum world stretching twisting curving
your small body to my own your hands
against my lips your fingers on my tongue

what is that sound what currency
is this what vessel for existing
ssssssshhhhhhhelllllllll

when you were still in shell   we counted you
in days   two cells on day one   four the second day
six the third   when you were placed

inside   another room   to make
your way an apple seed   a blueberry   an ear
of corn   a coconut   the day of shelling

came & went   till two weeks   on you flexed
we were two Sauls   something like scales
something like shells   were falling

from our eyes   as out you came
you come out with a cry just like the aaaaaaaahhhhhhhhhhh
of apple

Acknowledgments

My sincere thanks to Jay Bernard, Kate Birch, Chris Gribble and Helen Ivory for reading my competition submission with care and seeing possibilities in the proposal. Thank you to Kate Birch and Dominic Christian for supporting the Commission. Thanks also to *Ink Sweat & Tears* and Café Writers for giving me the opportunity to make this book and for support along the way.

Thank you to Emily Berry for publishing 'Untitled / Villanelle' in *The Poetry Review*, for suggesting I rethink the original title and for commissioning an accompanying 'Behind the Poem' essay for The Poetry Society website. My thanks to Mike Sims for publication assistance. Thank you to Madeline Potter for publishing 'Cuttlefish' in *Eborakon*.

I am grateful to the Arts Council of Northern Ireland for an award which has helped support the development of this book, and in particular to Damian Smyth for his ongoing support. Thank you to everyone at the Tyrone Guthrie Centre at Annaghmakerrig. Thank you to Margo McNulty for the beautiful cyanotype.

For their good writing, good conversation and encouragement I am deeply grateful to Vahni Capildeo, Ciaran Carson, Colin Graham, Donika Kelly, Alice Lyons, Sandra Newman, Adam Phillips and Ian Sansom.

Thank you to Erin, Matt, Moyra and Paul for reading as things took shape. My thanks to Jean for the hints.

Thank you to my fothermathers, living and dead.

And, most importantly, my thanks and love to Beth.

Gail McConnell is a poet, literary critic and Senior Lecturer in English at Queen's University Belfast. She is the author of *Northern Irish Poetry and Theology* (Palgrave, 2014) and articles on Irish and British poetry. Gail's first poetry pamphlet is *Fourteen* (Green Bottle Press, 2018) and she is working on a book featuring 'Type Face', a long poem published in *Blackbox Manifold* concerning her experience of reading a Historical Enquiries Team Report about her father's killing. Gail's poems have appeared in *Poetry Review*, *PN Review*, *Virginia Quarterly Review* and *Stand*, and she is the recipient of two Arts Council Northern Ireland awards. A programme based on *Fothermather* will be produced by Conor Garrett and broadcast on Radio 4 in 2020.